T0402872

by Charis Mather

Minneapolis, Minnesota

Credits

All images are courtesy of Shutterstock.com, unless otherwise specified. With thanks to Getty Images, Thinkstock Photo, and iStockphoto. Front Cover – NotionPic, EgudinKa, Naddya, aShatilov, VectorShow. 4–5 – Christopher Edwin Nuzzaco, Gearstd, Paleka. 6–7 – Sergey Nivens, Napat, nexus 7, r.classen, Ollyy, MaeManee. 8–9 – Utthapon wiratepsupon, Artemida-psy, Stefano Spicca, Anita Ponne, LeManna. 10–11 – Louid Rhead (via Wikimedia Commons), N. C. Wyeth (via Wikimedia Commons), Nigel Homer (via Wikimedia Commons), Peyker, SergeyKPI. 12–13 – John P Coates (via Wikimedia Commons), Albina Gavrilovic, Oleksandr_U, Ukki Studio, Erbsensuppe. 14–15 –Whitevector, sportpoint, ShutterSparrow, RICpaint (via Wikimedia Commons). 16–17 – alphaspirit.it, Julien Tromeur, Khosro, Vadim Zakharishchev. 18–19 – Charles Temple Dix (via Wikimedia Commons), FOTOKITA, Kris Mari, Vlad Podvorny, xpixel. 20–21 – Alexandr Chumakov, Alones, EvgeniiAnd, Kittyfly, Nidvoray. 22–23 – Ed Uthman (via Wikimedia Commons), Bojan Pavlukovic, Dan Kosmayer, Ollie Atkins (via Wikimedia Commons), RCA Records (via Wikimedia Commons), wavebreakmedia. 24–25 – Jarvin-Kjell (via Wikimedia Commons), LeeSensei, Olivier Le Moal, Powell F. Krueger. 26–27 – Andrii Iemelianenko, Alan Fisher (via Wikimedia Commons), GCapture, Janeness, Lifestyle Travel Photo, maradon 333, Notto Yeez. 28–29 – Carel L. de Vogel (via Wikimedia Commons), Dean Drobot, Edhubbard (via Wikimedia Commons). 30 – Shift Drive.

Bearport Publishing Company Product Development Team

President: Jen Jenson; Director of Product Development: Spencer Brinker; Managing Editor: Allison Juda; Associate Editor: Naomi Reich; Associate Editor: Tiana Tran; Senior Designer: Colin O'Dea; Associate Designer: Elena Klinkner; Associate Designer: Kayla Eggert; Product Development Specialist: Anita Stasson

Library of Congress Cataloging-in-Publication Data is available at www.loc.gov or upon request from the publisher.

ISBN: 979-8-88822-001-6 (hardcover)
ISBN: 979-8-88822-185-3 (paperback)
ISBN: 979-8-88822-316-1 (ebook)

For more information, write to Bearport Publishing, 5357 Penn Avenue South, Minneapolis, MN 55419.

CONTENTS

Welcome to TNT

TOTALLY NOT TRUE

There are some pretty crazy stories about people. But are they too crazy to be real? When it gets hard to know what to believe, we can always use science to explode stories that aren't true.

Some of the strangest stories seem to have **evidence** backing them. Let's **investigate** to find the truth.

We can use the scientific method to learn about things we don't understand. It helps us find out what we can trust.

The Scientific Method

The scientific method uses these steps.

STEP 1: Ask a question.

Does my teacher have eyes on the back of his head?

STEP 2: Make a guess.

Yes. He always catches me being silly.

STEP 3: Find evidence.

I did something silly when a hat was covering the back of his head, and he still caught me.

STEP 4: Answer your question.

He must have another way to see me.

STEP 5: Ask a new question and do it again.

Does he have spies? More investigation needed!

Warning! Some evidence in this book may be misleading or have a different explanation. Look out for this stamp.

LET'S GET EXPLODING!

Brainpower!

Some people believe we use only 10 percent of our brains. They think if we used more brainpower, we could do amazing things. People who believe this point to certain evidence.

Brain Buzz

Scientist Karl Lashley once used electricity to test different parts of the brain. He noticed that some areas seemed to do nothing.

TOTALLY USELESS!

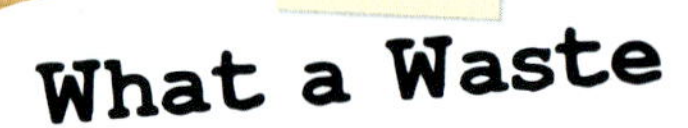

What a Waste

Brains are made up of many tiny cells. Only 1 out of every 10 cells is used for thinking. What are the other cells doing?

That's 10 percent!

Mega Memories

Some people's memories are so good they can remember every word in a book. They seem to never run out of space in their brains for new information.

Is most of our brain empty and waiting to be filled?

Language Unlocked

Have some people already unlocked more of their brainpower? There are reports of people who have woken up speaking a language they didn't speak before!

FOR MOST PEOPLE, IT TAKES YEARS TO LEARN A NEW LANGUAGE.

TIME TO BLOW UP ALL THE MISLEADING EVIDENCE WITH SCIENCE!

New and Improved

Since Lashley's test, scientific **equipment** has gotten better. Scientists now know we use all of our brains—even the parts that Lashley believed did nothing. Different parts of the brain work at different times.

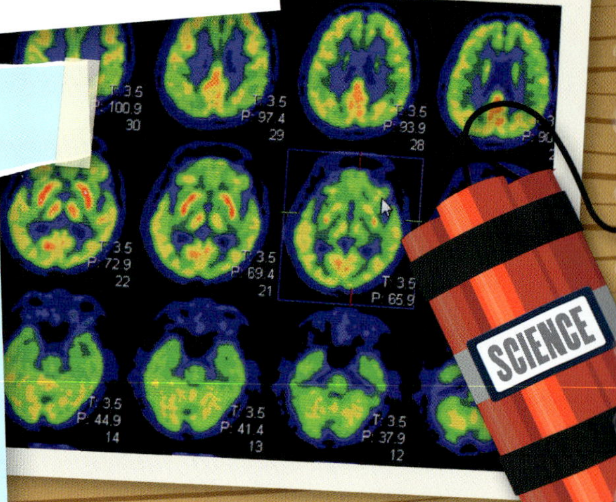

OUTDATED EVIDENCE CAN BE WRONG. WE SHOULD ALWAYS LOOK FOR THE LATEST EVIDENCE WHEN INVESTIGATING.

Cells at Work

There are actually two main types of cells in your brain. They are helper cells and thinking cells. You need both for your brain to work!

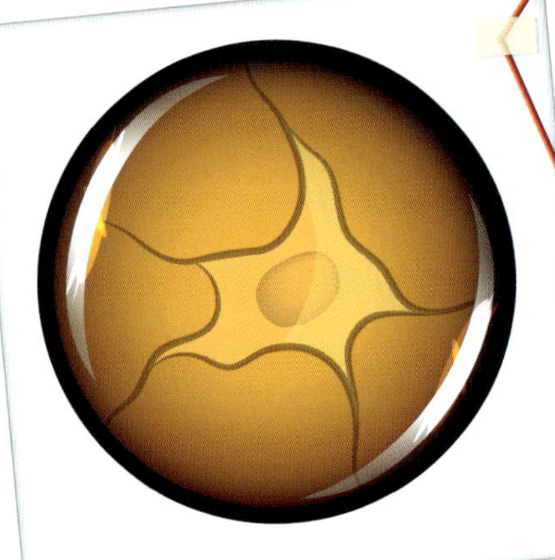

A THINKING CELL

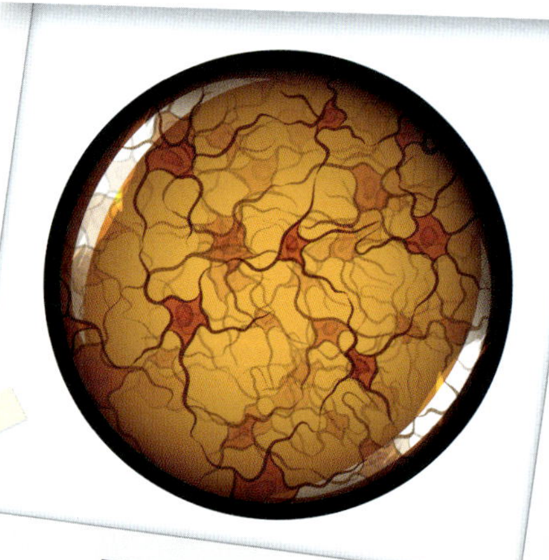

A HELPER CELL

Connected

Our brains are never really empty or full. Instead, they store memories by making connections between different parts of the brain. You can remember who people are because your brain made a connection between their names and faces.

SMARTER PEOPLE HAVE MORE CONNECTIONS IN THEIR BRAINS!

Brainy Back-Up

Different parts of the brain have different jobs. One part is in charge of language. If that part of the brain gets hurt, it might change how a person speaks. While the brain heals, it may switch to another language that it knows a little bit of. The other language is usually not spoken perfectly, even though it might sound like it.

Robin Hood

Many people have heard stories about the **outlaw** Robin Hood. He used his skills with a bow and arrow to steal from the rich and give to the poor. What we don't know is whether or not he was a real person.

Dead Shot

There is a grave with Robin Hood's name on it. As the stories go, he shot an arrow from his sickbed. He wanted to be buried at the place where it landed.

HIS FINAL SHOT?

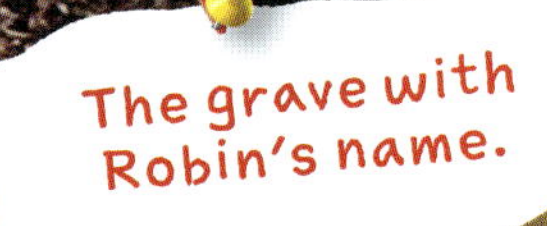

The grave with Robin's name.

A Rogue by Any Other Name

There are historical records of people with similar names to Robin Hood, such as Robyn Hod. Some of these records talk about the person being an outlaw or in jail, just like the stories!

This story is about someone named Robyn Hode

SPELLING WASN'T IMPORTANT DURING THE TIME ROBIN HOOD WAS ALIVE, SO ONE NAME MAY HAVE BEEN SPELLED MANY WAYS.

The Silver Arrow

Some stories tell of Robin winning a silver arrow. In 2021, an old arrow was found in a river near where Robin was said to have lived.

What an old silver arrow might have looked like.

The arrow from the river looked like this.

Same arrow?

LET'S EXPLODE SOME MISLEADING EVIDENCE!

Shot Down

The grave with Robin's name is more than 2,000 feet (600 m) from where Robin Hood was said to have died. Bows from that time were not strong enough to shoot that far. The grave probably doesn't belong to the Robin Hood from the stories.

Where Robin Hood was supposed to have died

A Buried Story

Could Robin's real grave be somewhere else? Investigators shot test arrows from the site of Robin's death. Some of the arrows landed almost exactly where an unnamed grave was found about 250 years ago. Maybe that's the real thing?

COULD THIS GRAVE HAVE BEEN ROBIN HOOD'S?

A Common Name

Most people who look at old records with the name Robin Hood think they aren't about the same person. When stories about the outlaw began, many people had names like Robynhood and Robinhud. Maybe one of them was the real guy, but maybe not.

Fool's Silver

The arrow tip was found by someone who was magnet fishing. The arrow was picked up out of the water by a strong magnet. But silver isn't magnetic! A silver arrow couldn't have been found this way.

Superstrength

Is it possible for humans to get superstrength? Let's look at some evidence that may say it's possible.

Polar Opposites

In Canada, a mother suddenly got superstrength when she had to fight off one of the biggest and strongest kinds of bear. A polar bear attacked Lydia Angyiou and her kids. She was somehow strong enough to fight back until help came.

Lydia was much smaller than the bear, but she was still able to keep her kids safe.

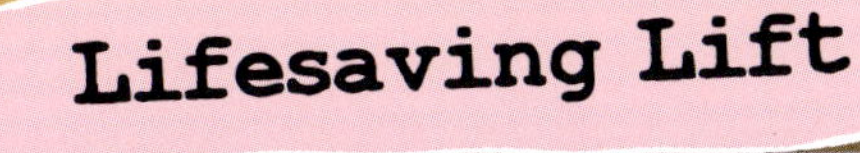

Lifesaving Lift

About 660 pounds (300 kg)

One man was trapped under his truck until his 19-year-old daughter was able to lift it and save him. Some of the strongest people in the world are able to **deadlift** a maximum of about 1,100 lbs (500 kg). Most trucks are more than twice as heavy as that. She must have had superstrength!

About 2,900 lbs (1,300 kg)

Berserk!

Viking berserkers were famous for their unusual strength. Berserkers were fighters who wore animal skins. During battle, they were said to become wild, angry, and superstrong—just like the animals whose skins they wore.

AS STRONG AS BEARS

ARE ANY EXPLOSIONS NEEDED HERE?

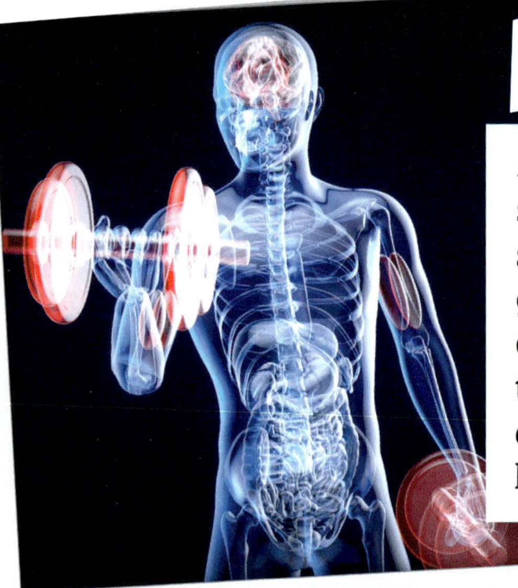

Grin and Bear It

Most of the time, our brains make sure we only use part of our strength to keep our muscles from getting hurt. In times of danger, our brains make chemicals that tell our bodies to ignore pain and work harder. That's what happened to Lydia Angyiou.

Emergency Chemicals

Some of these chemicals are adrenaline and endorphins. They make the body work harder and faster than normal. They also help your body feel less pain.

Both chemicals helped Lydia use more of the strength in her muscles.

Only Part of the Story

People who have lifted cars to save others usually lifted only part of the vehicles. Most of a car's weight was in the parts still touching the ground. Lifting just part of a car is amazing, but it doesn't require superstrength.

Wild to Weak

Berserkers really did exist, but their strength was not so super. Some people think berserkers might have eaten a dangerous plant just before battles that changed the way they fought. After the battles, the beserkers lost their strength.

NOT SO STRONG NOW!

FACT

Ghosts

Some people blame ghosts when there are unexplained sounds or movements. Let's look at some evidence that makes people think ghosts may be real.

HAUNTED BY GHOSTS?

Spooky Spots

Some houses might be haunted! There are places that can make people feel nervous, unwell, or uncomfortable without any reason. Are people being spooked by ghosts they can't see?

SOME PEOPLE SAY HOUSES BECOME HAUNTED BECAUSE PEOPLE HAVE DIED IN THEM.

Seeing Is Believing?

Ghosts may have been caught on camera. A picture of this ghostly shape was taken in Raynham Hall more than 200 years after Lady Dorothy Walpole died there.

LADY WALPOLE?

Ghost-hunting Gear

Ghost hunters use special equipment to test places they think might be haunted. Sometimes, this equipment gives strange readings, such as beeps or flashes, when it detects unexplained sounds or cold spots. It may pick up strange voices.

Ghost-hunting equipment

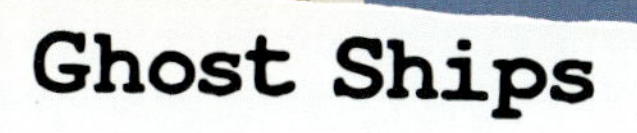

Ghost Ships

Sailors sometimes see ships that look like they are floating above the water out at sea. Are they ghost ships?

FLOATING!

Sailors in the past wrote about a ghost ship called *The Flying Dutchman*. One sailor who spotted it fell from the top of his ship and died soon after!

LET'S GET EXPLODING WITH SCIENCE!

Infrasound

The uncomfortable feeling people sometimes have in houses may be caused by **infrasound** rather than ghosts. This is a hum that is too low to hear, but it can still make people feel strange. Many normal things can cause infrasound, including electrical equipment and some kinds of weather.

Exposed!

Experts can make images similar to the ghost photo from Raynham Hall. It's done with a camera trick called long **exposure**. This is when part of the camera is left open for a long time to capture a photo.

MOVEMENT DURING A LONG EXPOSURE CAN MAKE THINGS LOOK GHOSTLY.

Evidence can be faked. Check it carefully!

The Wrong Tools for the Job

The tools ghost hunters use were not originally meant for ghost-hunting. When equipment is used for something other than what it's meant for, its readings can't be used as evidence. In fact, strange readings should be expected if equipment isn't used correctly!

YOU WOULDN'T TRY TO TELL HOW HOT A ROOM WAS WITH A CALCULATOR! MAKE SURE TO USE THE RIGHT EQUIPMENT TO GATHER EVIDENCE.

An optical illusion on land

Not a Match

Any sailor spotting a ghost ship is likely seeing an **optical illusion**. When light goes through air that is different temperatures, it can bend and make things appear to float, wiggle, or even look upside down!

EXPLODED BY SCIENCE!

Elvis Presley

STILL ALIVE?

Elvis Presley was a world-famous singer. When he died, many people didn't believe it. Some people even think he faked his death. What evidence do they have?

Did Presley leave America?

Singer Sighting

Soon after the news of Presley's death, someone said they spotted him at an airport buying a ticket to South America!

Face the Truth

The middle name on Presley's gravestone is spelled *Aaron*. But his family usually spelled it *Aron*. Did Presley leave a clue so his fans would know he was still alive?

Elvis Presley, FBI

Presley was once offered a job with the federal government. They asked him to stop bad people. He was even given an **FBI** badge. The bad people might have wanted to hurt Presley for helping the FBI. Faking his own death would have been a good way to hide from them.

Presley with President Nixon

Cover-Up

The three doctors looking into Presley's death may have lied about how he died. At first, they told people that his heart failed. Later, people found out this wasn't the whole story. Did the doctors get their story mixed up because Presley wasn't really dead?

TIME FOR TNT!

Was the airport Elvis just someone who looked like him?

Flight of Fancy

There's no record of Presley buying an airplane ticket or even a record of who first said he did! Don't trust stories without any evidence to back them up.

NOT ELVIS!

One investigator said the airport didn't even sell tickets to other countries that year!

Aaron's the Name

Later in his life, Presley wanted to use the spelling *Aaron* instead of *Aron*. He signed some official records using the middle name Aaron. Presley's family used the spelling he preferred on his gravestone.

from Elvis ??? Presley

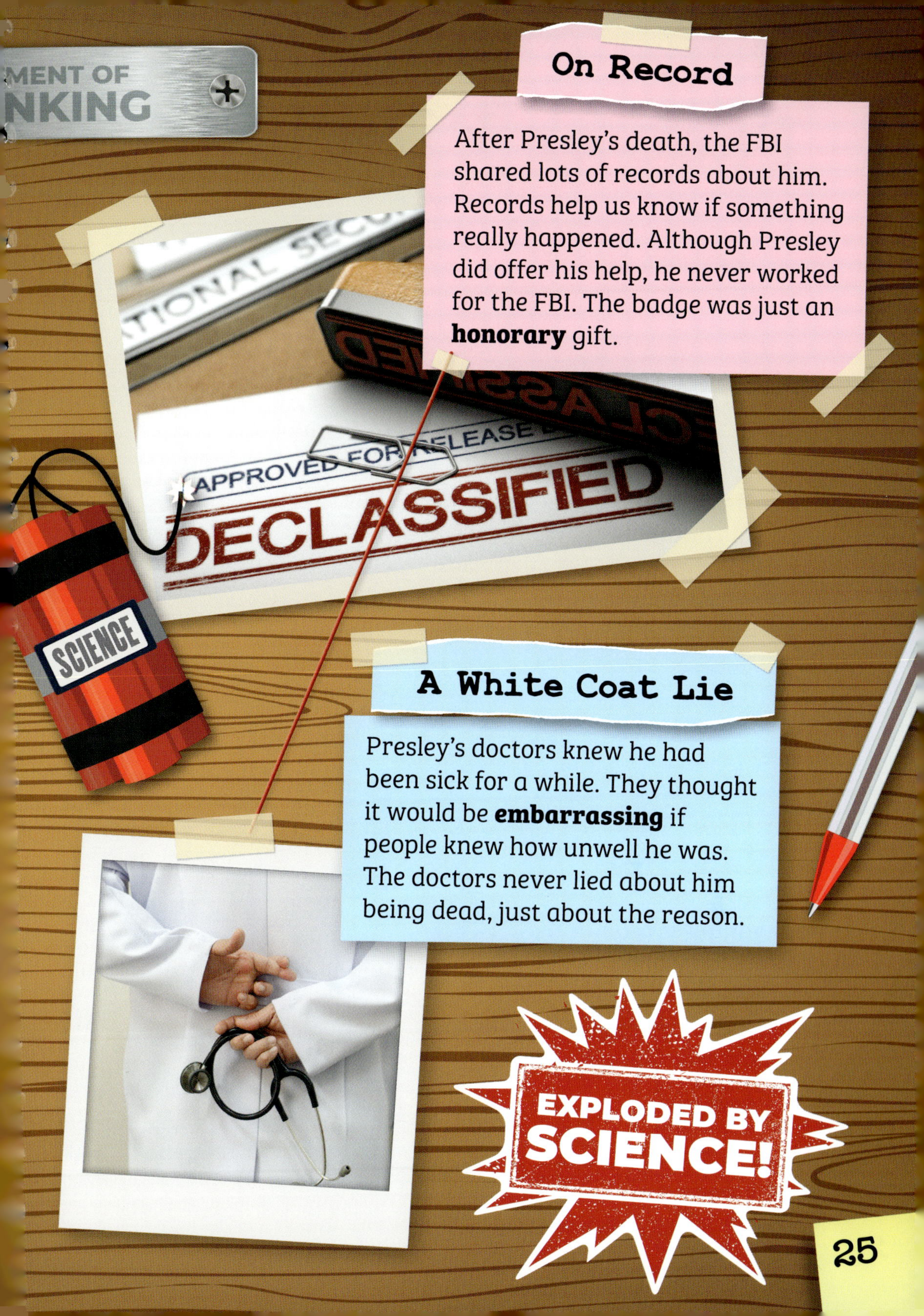

On Record

After Presley's death, the FBI shared lots of records about him. Records help us know if something really happened. Although Presley did offer his help, he never worked for the FBI. The badge was just an **honorary** gift.

A White Coat Lie

Presley's doctors knew he had been sick for a while. They thought it would be **embarrassing** if people knew how unwell he was. The doctors never lied about him being dead, just about the reason.

Fact or Fiction?

WOULD YOU BELIEVE ANY OF THESE STORIES?

Carrot Night Vision

During World War II (1939–1945), British pilots were surprisingly good at flying at night. They could even stop enemy airplanes in complete darkness! The British government said eating lots of carrots helped the pilots see in the dark.

MISLEADING WARNING EVIDENCE

Vampires

Are vampires real? There are stories about people whose skin would burn quickly in sunlight. Sometimes, their bodies were found with blood around their mouths after they died!

Walt Disney

Walt Disney is famous for making cartoons. Some people believe his body was frozen when he died. People who have their bodies frozen may hope to be made alive and healthy again when medical equipment gets better in the future.

Chilling!

Swapped Senses

We usually see with our eyes, hear with our ears, and taste with our tongues. Is it possible for some people to smell sounds? Can others see colors when looking at different letters? About 1 in every 2,000 people believe they can do something like this.

Must sniff out the truth!

WHICH TOTALLY-NOT-TRUE STORIES CAN WE EXPLODE?

Kept in the Dark

Carrots are good for your eyes but not that good! New **radar** equipment is what actually helped British soldiers see. But the government didn't want their enemies to know about the technology. So, they made up the carrot story.

Posters like this helped spread the story.

EXPLODED BY SCIENCE!

Put to Rest

Some **diseases** can make people's skin burn in sunlight. And some early doctors thought drinking animal blood might help people with the disease. It didn't, but now we know why people think vampires drink blood!

Thin Ice

The story of Disney's frozen body was probably made up by people who didn't know him very well. His own daughter said that he'd probably never even heard you could freeze your body after death.

DISNEY'S DEATH RECORDS DON'T MENTION HIM BEING FROZEN.

True Colors

Seeing, tasting, smelling, or hearing things with the wrong sense is called synesthesia. We can see how synesthesia works by scanning a person's brain while they are using their senses. It's real!

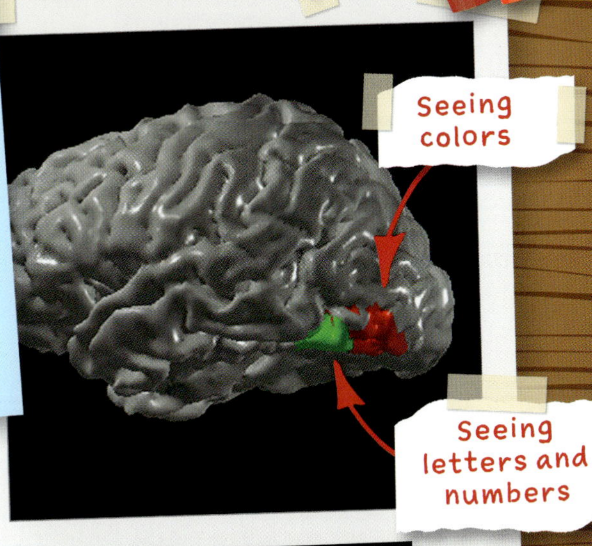

RIGHT NEXT TO EACH OTHER

WHEN LOTS OF PEOPLE ALL SAY THE SAME THING, WE SHOULD INVESTIGATE.

Sorted by Science

Stories about people suddenly getting superstrength may sound unbelievable even though they may be true. Other times, things that sound real may just be made up.

The scientific method is a great tool that helps us know when things are totally not true. With science, you can blow silly stories to pieces.

Next time you hear a story that you aren't sure about, don't just believe it. Put your science skills to the test. *Kaboom!*

GLOSSARY

deadlift a weight training exercise where you lift something off the ground and bring it to the level of your hips

diseases illnesses

embarrassing experiencing something that makes you feel like you did something silly

equipment the tools and machines needed to do a job

evidence objects or information that can be used to prove whether something is true

exposure the total amount of light allowed to fall on film when a photograph is taken

FBI Federal Bureau of Investigation; a part of the U.S. government that looks into crimes

honorary something meant to show respect

infrasound a type of sound that is lower than humans can hear

investigate to search for information about something

optical illusion something that tricks the eyes into seeing an image or pattern that isn't there

outdated not current

outlaw a criminal who is running away from the law

radar a system that uses radio waves to find moving objects in the sky

Viking a Norseman warrior or pirate who lived from the late 700s to about 1100

INDEX

READ MORE

Finn, Peter. *Do Ghosts Exist? (Fact or Fiction?).* New York: Gareth Stevens Publishing, 2022.

Goldstein, Margaret J. *What Are Conspiracy Theories? (Fake News).* Minneapolis: Lerner Publications, 2020.

Iyer, Rani. *The Science of Super Strength and Super Speed (The Science of Superpowers).* New York: Cavendish Square, 2019.

LEARN MORE ONLINE

1. Go to **www.factsurfer.com** or scan the QR code below.
2. Enter "**Not True People**" into the search box.
3. Click on the cover of this book to see a list of websites.